PLANT BASED DIET FOR BEGINNERS

Healthy, Pure & Delicious, The Natural
Way to Look and Feel Your Best

SUSAN ELLERBECK

Disclaimer

This information is not intended to provide medical advice or to take the place of medical advice and treatment. Readers are strongly advised to consult a qualified medical professional regarding the treatment of medical conditions. The author and publisher shall not be held liable or responsible for any misunderstanding or misuse of the information contained in this guide or for any loss, damage, or injury caused or alleged to be caused directly or indirectly by any information, treatment, action, or application of any food or food source discussed in this guide. This information is general and is offered with no guarantees on the part of the authors or publisher. This information is not intended to diagnose, treat, cure, or prevent any disease. Nothing in the guide is to be considered personal, legal, or professional advice.

CONTENTS

INTRODUCTION

Our health as a nation is in a sorry state of affairs. According to the CIA World Factobook, the USA ranks 50th for life expectancy. This is a direct result of the Standard American Diet.

Indeed, because of our poor lifestyle and dietary choices, our bodies have turned against us. The direct result of this rebellion is sickness and chronic disease. There is hope, however.

By changing the way we eat, we can reverse the damage we have inflicted on our bodies. We can counter years of nutritional deficiency by eating plant based whole foods.

In switching to a plant based diet, the body can be brought back into balance, and begin the process of healing itself. The simple truth is eating a plant based diet lowers your risk of many diseases, including heart disease and cancer.

This guide will look at the plant based diet, all its benefits, and what is involved in making the switch. In the end you will gain a working knowledge of how to use plant based foods to your own advantage, and how to enjoy a whole new type of delicious cuisine.

Lets begin!

WHY PLANTS?

Indeed, because of our poor lifestyle and dietary choices, our bodies have turned against us. The direct result of this rebellion is sickness and chronic disease. There is hope, however.

By changing the way we eat, we can reverse the damage we have inflicted on our bodies. We can counter years of nutritional deficiency by eating plant based whole foods.

In switching to a plant based diet, the body can be brought back into balance, and begin the process of healing itself. The simple truth is eating a plant based diet lowers your risk of many diseases, including heart disease and cancer.

This guide will look at the plant based diet, all its benefits, and what is involved in making the switch. In the end you will gain a working knowledge of how to use plant based foods to your own advantage, and how to enjoy a whole new type of delicious cuisine.

Lets begin!

In the modern world we have an overwhelming array of food options. Western diets can be made up of almost anything we choose. Just consider the different types of cuisine available - any day of the week you could eat

"Italian", "Thai", "Tex-Mex", and "fast" food among dozens of other varieties.

There are also the specific "diets" that millions follow as well - the "Grapefruit Diet", the many different "cleansing" diets, the specific eating plans such as the "Jenny Craig" line of pre-package weight loss foods, and so on.

We also eat diets that are built around specific groups of food - we are meat loving carnivores, egg and cheese eating vegetarians, plant-only eating vegans, etc.

Obviously, with all of these choices, and with so much information and misinformation floating around, understanding how to eat the healthiest way can be difficult to determine. In fact, simply finding the answer to the question of: "What is the healthiest way to eat?" may seem like an impossible feat.

Fortunately, many authors, food experts, and researchers have come up with a fairly simple answer, but for different reasons (which we will look at shortly). Basically, their many theories add up to the following method for healthy eating at its best:

1. Eat whole food.
2. Don't eat a lot of food.
3. Try to eat mostly plants.
4. Eat seasonally when it is possible.
5. Don't eat anything you cannot pronounce.

That's it, and that describes the "Plant Based Diet" that this book is all about. However, this leads us to another question, which is: "Why plants?"

UNDERSTANDING THE PLANT BASED DIET

We live in a society where we have epidemics in obesity and diabetes, we are plagued by chronic diseases, and cancer rates have shot through the roof. While many of us are obese, we are also undernourished. We are eating processed foods on a daily basis and these foods have been depleted of practically all nutrients. We are fat and starving at the same time. Our children are also affected and today we have more obese children than at any time in history. All of these health problems can be tied to the Standard American Diet (SAD).

Before the modern age of processed foods began, most people at fresh fruits and vegetables on a daily basis. Meat was not eaten daily and when it was it was accompanied by a healthy serving of vegetables. Indeed, in those days people understood the health benefits of plant foods, which is why children were often reminded to eat their greens. This was good advice. Those green vegetables are powerhouses of nutrition. They are loaded with not only vitamins and minerals, but vital enzymes and proteins as well.

Recent medical studies (like The China Study, and the work of Caldwell Esselstyn) show the amazing health benefits of a plant based diet. The China Study showed direct links between the amount of meat eaten and cancer rates, and further displayed how people living on plant based diets saw very low rates of cancer. The clinical work of Caldwell Esselstyn showed that a plant based diet can not only help prevent heart disease, but that a plant based diet can also reverse heart disease and repair damaged arteries. A famous example of this is former President Bill Clinton who after ongoing battles with heart disease adopted Dr. Esselstyn's plant based diet and over several months saw his heart disease start to reverse. President Clinton has also lost weight on the diet and says he "feels great".

While many people follow a plant based diet in order to drop some weight, they simultaneously lower their cholesterol, balance their blood sugar, and even lower blood pressure by eliminating the meat, dairy, and processed foods. When you eliminate meat and dairy, you also reduce the risks of many types of cancers and other chronic diseases.

Remember that a plant based diet rarely relies on pre-packaged foods that are full of unknowable chemicals and many hidden animal-based products. Instead, the true plant based diet uses nutrient dense whole foods that are combined to create delicious and well-balanced meals.

Improving your health is a very strong argument in favor of a plant based diet, but there is also an environmental argument. In June of 2010, the United Nations issued a report that said that the world's greenhouse gas problem is related directly to the use of fossil fuels, but pointed out that agriculture (particularly the raising of meat and dairy products) was an equally serious part of the problem.

The report really only validated what others had been saying all along, and that is that the meat and dairy industries consume and burn tons of fossil fuels as they raise food crops for animals, grow the animals, transport meat and products over long distances, and generally harm the environment every step of the way. For example, some studies have indicated that animal-based agriculture is responsible for around 18% of all greenhouse gas production. This is pretty substantial when you also read that all of the world's forms of transportation create less than 14% of greenhouse emissions.

Additionally, one resource indicated that the U.S. Geological Survey determined that it can take up to 18,000 gallons of water to raise the amount of meat needed in a single hamburger patty!

So, the positive environmental impacts alone are a good reason to consider shifting away from commercially produced meats and dairy foods. If we eliminate industrial foods from our diet, we certainly shrink the size of our own carbon footprint because we are not participating in the use of fossil fuels or wasting energy.

THE REALITY OF PLANT BASED EATING

Many people groan at the thought of switching to a plant based diet because they automatically envision piles of leafy greens and carrots on their plates, and while that could be quite delicious; the plant based diet is actually much more complex than most realize. Just consider the following foods consumed in a traditional plant based eating plan:

- Fruits of all kinds;
- Veggies of all kinds;
- Grains like quinoa, hemp, and brown rice;
- Nuts and seeds of all kinds;
- Meat alternatives like smoked tempeh, tofu, and seitan;
- Beans of all kinds;
- Breads and baked goods of many kinds;
- Cereals;
- Nut butters; and
- Oils, vinegars, spices, and seasonings.

Obviously, that list goes on much longer, but is given as a simple demonstration of the huge variety of foods, and the endless combinations that are possible when you cut back on the dairy and the meat.

Something to keep in mind, however, is that a plant based diet can easily go astray too. There are some folks who eat white flours, sugary foods, and processed or fried foods that are just as bad as the meat-based meals and diets. This simply means that someone who is hoping to eat the healthiest way possible and to follow a plant based diet will need to consider the following factors:

- Calories;

- Fat;

- Fiber; and

- Source of the food.

These are things we are going to consider in the next chapter, and we are also going to look at the best ways to make the change from a meat based diet to one that relies mostly, or entirely, on plant based foods instead.

We will consider the many benefits of unprocessed (also called "whole") foods, and how to convert your diet into one that is far different from the SAD or the Standard American Diet. We will look at the foods you can and should eat, explore a few different menus and recipes, and generally discover that a plant based diet is delicious, healthful, and actually fun and easy to follow!

So, if you are ready to begin, let's start with a look at the content of foods and how to begin choosing the right items for your daily diet.

MAKING THE BEST FOOD CHOICES

Though there is now a lot of talk about a global obesity issue, there is also a great deal of good eating going on as well. Consider that it is estimated that roughly 27% of all restaurant customers request a vegetarian option, and that around ten percent of the United States population claims to be vegetarian of some kind or another (meaning that they are lacto-ovo, vegan, semi-vegetarian, etc.).

learly, this means that a lot of people have already started to make the change to a plant based diet, but that does not necessarily mean that they are all making ideal food choices. Though it is not at all common to see a true vegetarian who is obese, the amount of processed foods now made specifically for those avoiding meat can often make it hard to choose wisely and stay slender. And you do want to choose wisely because making the same mistakes in plant based foods as you have with animal based foods eliminates the many benefits gained.

Consider that you would lose out on the cholesterol reducing properties of whole grains and a low fat diet, the hypertension eliminating properties of low sodium and natural foods, and the blood sugar regulating qualities of high fiber and low sugar natural foods!

For example, it is very easy to find all kinds of pre-packaged meat substitutes, and some are full of fat, carbohydrates, sugars, and fillers. The same can be said about frozen vegetarian or vegan meals, vegan friendly baked goods, and more.

This means that it is a good idea to begin to transition into a plant based diet by understanding such things as caloric requirements, fat, and more. In other words, it is time to become a label reader when you buy packaged foods.

It is also imperative to understand the "nature" of food, meaning simply that a plant based diet is one that should follow the seasons. For example, if you live in New England you would not be naturally able to enjoy a bowl of field fresh strawberries in the middle of January. This is due to the simple fact that it is not their "season" in that part of the world.

If you want to use the plant based diet to enjoy the most nutritious whole foods and to become a more environmentally friendly eater, it is a wise idea to also recognize the need to eat seasonally, locally, and from farmers who try to be as organic and responsible as possible.

Let's take some time to consider these issues in a bit more depth.

Understand Calories, Fat, Fiber, and the Source of Food

Calories...it is a word that dieters may come to dislike, but it is also just the technical term that explains the energy potential in any source of food. Thus, you NEED to eat calories in order to get energy and to survive, but many of us are unsure of the actual number of calories required to keep our bodies working, and the kinds of calories to consume.

For instance, we hear often about "empty calories," and these are calories supplied by foods like processed white sugar and solid fat. The SAD contains many of these calories (too many of them), which provide almost no nutrition and which are used and stored by the body in the most harmful ways. It is okay to eat some empty calories each day, but to allow the vast majority of the daily diet to be composed of them will tend to make the individual overweight and prone to illness.

The plant based diet can easily help to avoid this empty calorie issue because plants are always nutrient dense, provide high quality calories, and contain no saturated fat. They are usually high in fiber and helpful in regulating blood sugar too.

Of course, just hearing about the plant based diet and its low calorie content is not that useful unless you know how many calories YOU need. Yes, each person requires a different number of calories. To determine this figure requires the use of the BMR (Basal Metabolic Rate) formula, which gives each individual their ideal calorie amount for any given day.

THE BMR

The thing to keep in mind about the BMR is that it is indicating the number of calories that you should consume each day while you remain entirely at rest. If you are active and burn off calories, you need to remember this and adjust your diet accordingly.

Here are the formulas for men and women, and we'll follow them with an example:

Adult females: 655 + (4.3 x weight in lbs.) + (4.7 x height in inches) - (4.7 x age in years); or

Adult males: 66 + (6.3 x body weight in lbs.) + (12.9 x height in inches) - (6.8 x age in years).

Here is an example of a 42 year old woman who is 5'7" tall and who weighs 145 pounds:

655 + 623.5 + 314.9 - 197.4 = 1396 calories per day while at rest.

So, this woman would need to eat 1400 calories per day to maintain her current weight, but only if she sat around most of the day and used very few of those calories. Additionally, around ten percent of the calories she would consume would be burned off in digestion alone. So, around 140 of those 1400 calories would go directly to metabolism.

That means the formula has to adjust upward and add the lost calories back into the equation, meaning that 1540 calories would be acceptable to maintain the current weight.

Clearly, this means she needs to eat more than that, but the actual figure would vary based on the amount of energy she used during her day.

Take some time right now to calculate your BMR. Remember to account for the ten percent directed towards digestion, and to try to determine how many calories you burn during any daily exercise or activity. Add this figure back into your calorie requirements if you are seeking to maintain your weight, but avoid adding these calories to the diet if you are trying to lose some weight.

Note: when seeking to lose weight you can use the BMR to determine how many calories needed, and then use exercise to create a "deficit". Be careful with weight loss, however, and seek to drop no more than two pounds per week.

WHAT IS IN THE CALORIES?

In addition to the total calorie count, you should understand how much of your daily diet has to be comprised of protein, fat, and carbohydrates too. This is actually a very easy set of figures to remember, and the current guidelines in the United States for average adults are:

- Carbohydrates: 45% – 65% of total calories

- Fat: 20 % - 35% of total calories

- Protein: 10% – 35% of total calories

This shows us how many of the daily calories should go to the various nutrients and compounds in food. These, however, are merely averages, and you may want to speak with a physician or nutritionist if you have any health concerns.

What do those percentages actually mean? Well, we can return to the woman who should eat between 1400 and 1540 calories per day. When she calculates her daily intake, it means she should be aiming for around 675 calories in carbs, 450 calories in fat, and 300 calories in protein.

Many people new to the plant based diet automatically worry about that ten to thirty-five percent of total calories in protein as well as the percentages of fat too. They fear that they won't be able to get their daily requirements from an all plant diet. These are unnecessary concerns because the plant based diet contains all of the nutrients and food sources that the body requires.

Fat, for example, in the plant based diet should come from quality sources, and is a bit easier to find than protein. Good sources of fat and calories in the plant based diet would include any nuts or seeds, olives and olive oil, vegetable oils and margarines, and plants like avocados.

Protein, is also not really a challenge when you have access to "perfect protein" combinations, like beans and rice, or any whole grains with nuts, seeds, beans, or even many fruits and vegetables. Don't forget that soy is used to create low fat tofu, soy milk, and other protein dense foods.

Carbohydrates are where fiber comes into the daily diet too, and it is important to understand the differences between complex and simple carbohydrates. Let's begin to do just that with a look at digestion.

CARBOHYDRATES AND THE BODY

When you eat any sort of carbohydrate, the body breaks down the starch into various types of "glucose" that the body may use right away for energy or store as fat. Many carbs also contain insoluble fiber, which is not something the body totally breaks down. Instead, it goes through the digestive tract and works to cleanse it out along the way.

The carbohydrates that come from starch and which are converted into glucose are often called "simple" carbs. The ones that come in the form of insoluble fiber are "complex" carbs.

To keep it very easy and basic: the simple carbs are those that are broken down in the digestive system and used almost immediately. The complex carbs are those that take a while to digest and which tend to be fiber dense, and full of nutrients.

The SAD is loaded with simple carbs such as white bread, white sugar, and lots of foods and additives that end with the letters "ose", such as sucrose, glucose, etc. These cause the body to produce insulin which forces the cells to store the excess glucose. Because the system is putting this glucose into the blood stream much faster than it can be used, the body stores it as fat. Thus, too many simple carbs lead to weight gain.

The good news in all of this is that the plant based diet is very high in the complex carbs that are found in foods such as veggies, whole grains, oatmeal, brown rice, beans, and whole wheat foods.

So, you now understand that you need fat, calories, carbs and more. You may also be starting to recognize the simple fact that a plant based diet can easily become one that requires you to consume a high volume of food in order to obtain daily nutrition. This is why it is a very wise idea to create custom eating plans and to choose the most nutrient dense foods possible.

FAT AND CHOLESTEROL

One of the best reasons and greatest benefits relating to the plant based diet is the elimination of the worst kinds of fat and cholesterol. These things really can disappear from the diet immediately because you will no longer consume the saturated fats that appear only in animal based food products.

Without getting into the technical details, if you simply eliminate foods like meat, butter, eggs, and cheese from your diet, you automatically reduce "bad" cholesterol levels. Additionally, the compounds in most plant based foods are known to further lower this "LDL" cholesterol in the blood stream as well. Studies showed that the "sterols" in plant based foods such as soy and psyllium husks dropped LDL levels by an additional ten percent or more.

That alone indicates the intelligence in the choice to switch over to the plant based eating plan. A bit later we look at eating plans, but right now we'll briefly discuss the right places and times to purchase many of the foods you will consume. We make a point of this because you will have to obtain foods of the highest quality in order to get the most nutrition from them.

EATING SEASONAL AND LOCAL FOODS

If you want food that contains the highest nutrient count and which provides the greatest benefits, you need to consider the source and the season. For instance, there will be a substantial difference in the nutrient value of a tomato taken from the vine that morning and eaten later in that same day compared to one picked green, gassed for ripening, and shipped across the country to be sold days or even weeks later.

This is a simple illustration of the benefits of shopping seasonally and locally. Remember that local and seasonal shoppers are also often going to also be able to eat organically grown food that was raised nearby, driven only a short distance, and kept in the healthiest conditions possible. This too boosts the nutrient content of the food too.

When you avoid commercially grown foods, you are also cutting the risks of ingesting what many call "frankenfoods" or genetically modified foods that are capable of meeting the demands of commercial farming, but which are not known to be the best for health and well being.

Of course, not all of your foods can be found at a local farmer's market, and you may not have the budget for it even if it is possible to get everything from the local farmers. In that case, you have to learn how to shop the supermarket in an optimal manner.

A MAP OF THE GROCERY STORE

How do you know that you are choosing the best foods when you are forced to shop in a modern supermarket? If you are mostly a "perimeter shopper," it is quite likely that you are eating a very healthy plant based diet.

Here is what we mean:

Walk into any modern, large grocery store and you are going to see that everything requiring refrigeration is located on the perimeter and not often in the aisles. Additionally, all of the produce, health food, baked goods, and seasonal products are located on the perimeter as well. Even things like freshly made pasta and "olive bars" are appearing in the perimeter areas too.

So, if you need only enter the aisles for things like bulk grains and dried legumes, it is quite likely that you are an optimal shopper. Just remember that label reading is a "must" when you pick up any pre-made or pre-packaged food.

BEGINNING TO CHANGE

All of this may seem like a lot if you are just beginning, and yet if you are already a relatively healthy eater it may seem fairly simple. The thing to remember is that you want to begin shopping in a way that reflects the needs of your new diet. This means making plans that include detailed shopping lists and a collection of recipes that you can use to ensure you get the appropriate calories and nutrients each day.

In the last chapter of this book we look at the various menus and recipes that are most often used by those following the plant based diet, and we also provide a list of the most commonly selected foods to help you get started filling up your pantry too.

Keep in mind that it would be ideal if you could shop at farmer's markets and buy only seasonal foods, but if that is not possible, just try to purchase organic when available and to be the best "perimeter shopper" you can.

Regardless of where you shop for foods, switching to a plant based diet is going to eliminate the "costs" of commercial growing/raising and the transportation of products. It will allow you to eat whole foods and get the most nutrients possible, and it can allow you to support a local agricultural system rather than a vast commercial entity that operates far away and in ways no environmentally friendly at all.

Note: even those who decide to become "flextarians" (semi-vegetarian) can choose seasonal and local farm goods, such as grass fed beef and cage free chickens, to ensure that the environment and the animals are not paying heavily for their consumer food choices.

Now that you know more about what you need from your foods, it is time to look at the individual food groups.

THE MANY PLANT BASED FOODS

Try to make a quick list of the "plant based foods" that you eat. You will probably mention such things as bananas, lettuce, tomatoes, and all kinds of other fruits and vegetables, but you must also add such things as seeds and beans, nuts, grains, and everything else that provides nutrition but does not come from an animal. Those veggie burgers you enjoy or the tofu hot dogs you put on the grill in the summer, are also going to fall under the heading of plant based food as well.

This means that using this method of eating actually opens up your daily diet to a tremendous range of options. For example, the person on a plant based diet could have buckwheat pancakes with blueberries for breakfast, TVP (texturized vegetable protein) chili with a corn biscuit and a green salad at lunch, a protein smoothie as an afternoon snack, and a massive pot of stir fry as their meal in the evening. There are almost no limits to the types of meals that a plant based diet can feature.

Additionally, there is always going to be the need to make that famous "rainbow on your plate" in order to get the calories and nutrients required, and so the many options available to the plant based eater are a real bonus.

CHOOSING FOOD

In order to be sure you understand just how diverse your diet can be, let's look at all of the primary food sources.

Before we take a peek at the list, however; let's briefly discuss the issue of food color as mentioned above. Health advocates have said that a colorful plate is one that is well balanced in terms of nutrients. Why do they say this? It is because foods contain "phytochemicals" that give them their different colors and which are actual the "bioactive" materials contained in the foods.

For example, we say that a food has antioxidants, and what we mean is that the food is high in specific phytochemicals that are beneficial to human health and wellness.

When you eat a plant based diet, it is useful to know what the color of any specific food might mean in terms of nutrition, and then try to fill your plate with as many of the beneficial compounds as possible. Below is a list of food colors and the phytochemicals that they are most known for providing.

- Pale green to white - Allicin, quercetin, and flavinoids are commonly found in foods that naturally have such hues. This group includes foods like green grapes, white grape juice, and the many kinds of onions such as leeks, chives, and even garlic.

- Green - The leafy greens are known for their indoles and sulforaphanes. This group includes kale, brussels sprouts, cabbages of all kinds, and broccoli, among others.

- Yellowish Green to Bright Yellow - Containing zeaxanthin and luetin, foods in this color range include some of the greens like spinach or collard and mustard greens, but also avocados, honeydew melon, corn on the cob, and peas of all kinds.

- Pale Yellow to Orange - This color is a good cue to high beta cryptothanxin content and is found in foods like peaches, oranges and orange juice, papaya, and tangerines.

- Bright Orange - The famous carotenoids (what people speak about when they are discussing beta carotene as a cancer fighting compound) are found in foods like carrots, pumpkins, mangos, cantaloupes, all of the hard skinned squashes such as butternut and acorn, and sweet potatoes.

- Red and Purple - This is the group in which anthrocyanins are found and include such richly hued foods as strawberries, grapes and grape juice, cranberries, red apples, blackberries, and even dried prunes.

- Bright Red - Another well known phytochemical is lycopene, and it is in high quantities in foods such as tomatoes and tomato products, watermelon, and even ruby red or pink grapefruit.

Go ahead and build a rainbow on your plate during each meal, or at least try to give yourself a small sampling of these highly beneficial compounds at each mealtime. For instance, a homemade fruit smoothie that uses greens and fruits is a good way to add "color" to your plate of less colorful foods such as rice and a protein source.

THE MAIN FOOD GROUPS

Now that you understand a bit more about nutrient value in your food, let's look at the many food groups you can use in your plant based diet.

- Greens - This is a category separate from the rest of the vegetables because greens, particularly dark and leafy greens of all kinds, are a primary source for many nutrients. For instance, a pot of steamed kale contains a huge amount of calcium, vitamins, and iron. Greens are known for offering protection from diabetes and heart disease as well as packing a lot of fiber into every serving. The most common greens for a plant based diet are the hearty varieties such as kale, broccoli and broccoli rabe, spinach, collards, chard, turnip greens, mustard greens, cabbage, and romaine lettuce, among others. The USDA recommends that adults over the age of 19 eat 2.5 or more cups of veggies each day, and so it would be good to aim for a full cup of greens every day if possible.

- Protein Sources - You don't have to "give in" and eat eggs or dairy products in order to get protein. The USDA provides an overwhelming list of foods that are used as protein sources, and though there are plenty of animal based foods on that list, there are also:

- All of the beans provide an impressive amount of protein in each serving, and good options include soy, lentils, kidney, black, garbanzo, pinto, lima, navy, white beans, and more. The soy beans are used to make another source of protein - tofu (also called bean curd), but also to make tempeh, TVP, soy yogurt, ice cream, cheese, and a great milk substitute.

- The many kinds of nuts and seeds are also great for protein content as well. You can eat almonds, walnuts, hazelnuts, pecans, cashews, peanuts, pistachios, pumpkin seeds, sunflower seeds, nut butters, sesame seeds, flax, and more.

- How much protein are you supposed to eat? Like all of the different food groups, it really depends on your age, gender, and level of activity. The safest range for adults over the age of 19 is around five to six ounces per day.

- Fruits - There are no limitations to the kinds of fruits that can be eaten when using a plant based diet, but these do tend to have higher sugar content and should always be eaten in moderation. The recommended daily serving of fruit food sources varies according to gender, age, and level of activity, but it is reasonable to say that adults over the age of 19 can aim for two cups of fruits each day. The more common fruits include apples, bananas, dried fruits like raisins or prunes, all of the citrus fruits, mangoes, oranges, peaches, pineapple, and many more. There are also all of the berries, the different kinds of melons, and even fruit juices. The "trick" to using fruit juice, however, is to use only the 100% fruit juice beverages and to read labels to be sure that they are not from concentrate and have no added sugars.

- Vegetables - In addition to the dark green and leafy vegetables mentioned above, a person on a plant based diet can eat a great many servings of vegetables each day. Just like fruit, however, there are some vegetables that contain sugar in the form of high starch content. For example, potatoes of all kinds are vegetables, but they are starchy vegetables that can lead to weight gain if eaten in large quantities. Vegetables can be viewed in the following "groups":

  - Starchy - Would include corn, plantain, peas, lima beans, potatoes, water chestnuts, cassava, and tar root.

  - Green vegetables - Leafy greens of all kinds, broccoli, and lettuces of all kinds.

  - Reds and Oranges - Tomatoes and tomato juice, carrots, orange fleshed squashes, red peppers, sweet potatoes, and yams.

  - Beans and Peas - Whether dried or fresh, these are a vegetable that has to be consumed in measured quantities in the same way that starchy vegetables must be monitored. They include all of the beans, lentils, fresh peas, and dried peas or beans.

  - All the rest - From artichokes and asparagus to bean sprouts and mushrooms, anything not listed above is considered to be among the rest of the vegetable group. Most of these can be eaten without limit, but keep in mind that any root vegetables (like beets or turnips) can be high in sugar content.

How many servings of vegetables are you supposed to eat daily? Like all of the different food groups, it is going to again depend on age, gender, and level of activity. The safest range for adults over the age of 19 is around two to three cups per day.

- Grains and Starches - The USDA views grains in two ways: as whole grains and as refined grains. If you want the most "bang for the buck" you should go for the whole grains as much as possible because they contain the entire grain kernel. This is where the bran is found and where the most nutrients are contained. Examples would include brown rice, whole cornmeal, amaranth, buckwheat, bulgur wheat, oatmeal, millet, popcorn, rolled oats, quinoa, whole grain barley, and whole wheat flour. You can also include whole wheat bread, crackers, and pasta in this list too.

How much to eat? Adults over the age of 19 will want at least six to eight ounces of grains daily, with a minimum of at least three of those ounces in whole grain form.

- Fats - Because the plant based diet does not contain the super saturated fats of animal meats and products (including dairy), it may seem like there are no concerns about fats, but you do need to keep track of them. Your body must have fat to function properly and yet you want to supply it with the best options available. That means using the following plant based sources:
  - "Butters" and margarines made from pure vegetable oil

38

- Nuts and seeds, or butters made from them

- Olives or olive oil

- Soybean products or soybean oil

- Vegetable based oils such as canola, corn, cottonseed, safflower, and sunflower oils

What is the daily allowance? Adults over the age of 19 should aim for five to seven teaspoons of fat or oil each day. That is a considerable amount, but a few tablespoon of peanut butter tossed into a smoothie or a salad with olive oil and avocado would also do the trick!

- All of the Rest - What else is left? Consider the many "other" food sources that plant based eaters include in their daily diets. For instance:

  - Herbal teas of all kinds, black tea, and coffee,

  - Spices that are used for both flavoring and health benefits,

  - Nutritional yeast, and even such compounds as spirulina/hemp/flaxseed powder that add nutrients to everything,

  - Miso paste is another good "other" food to have on hand as well,

  - Vinegars (especially cider, red wine, and balsamic) and other fermented foods to supply you with lots of good, natural "flora",

  - Coconut milk and nut milks to enhance lots of different foods such as soups and hot beverages,

- ○ Many plant based eaters also drink wine or beer, and use it to enhance the flavors of some cooked foods, and

- ○ Don't forget the many fresh and dried herbs that add fiber, flavor, and nutrients.

Looks like you're not so limited after all, right? In fact, you could pick up almost any kind of cookbook and find ways to adjust many of the recipes to a purely plant based version thanks to the availability of so many good food sources.

The key to success, however, is to begin to make the transition from a vegetarian or meat eating diet to the purely plant based version. To do this takes a bit of time and effort, but is one of the best methods for success. Many people find that just eliminating all of the meat and dairy at one time is too difficult and will often find themselves eating meat full time. Others find the shift from white flour and sugar to entirely whole grain a challenge too.

What all of this means is fairly simple - to move into the plant based diet requires a gradual shift. To do that means becoming a "flexitarian" first, and then transitioning fully into the plant based way of eating. This is what we look at in the next chapter.

FLEXITARIANS

Though the word "flexitarian" only entered "proper" vocabulary in 2012 (the first year it appeared in the Merriam Webster Collegiate Dictionary), it was in use for more than a decade before that. It is meant to describe someone who eats in a sort of semi-vegetarian way. For example, the formal definition provided in the Dictionary is: "A vegetarian who occasionally eats meat."

Even within that definition, however, are further definitions. There are the "pollotarians" who eat poultry and fowl, the "pescetarians" who consume fish, and the combined "pesc-pollotarians" who eat both fish and poultry, but who avoid red meat of any kind (i.e. beef, pork, etc.).

This means that it may be easier for you to commit first to becoming a successful flexitarian of some kind or another before shifting entirely into a plant based diet. You can do so while also keeping in line with the environmental, humanitarian, and health goals of the fully plant based diet as well.

For example, consider the following suggestions for flexitarians:

1. Read labels and understand food sources - If you are struggling to cut out all meat and dairy, at least read packaging labels and understand who you are purchasing from. The local farmer's market is the best way to cut the environmental costs of meat. This farmer is likely to offer pasture raised animals who ate their natural diets and lived in clean and humane conditions. They would have been slaughtered in an efficient and cruelty-free manner and the processing would be minimal. The meat would come from only a short distance and be of the highest quality imaginable. The same can be said for the dairy and eggs from such operations as well.

2. Go for organic - No matter what you are eating (meat, dairy, produce, baked goods, etc.) consider investing exclusively in organic foods. Free range chickens, eggs, and beef cattle are often raised in an organic way too, and you should really support farmers dedicated to this approach to animal farming.

3. Vegetarian and cage free eggs - If you have not found it possible to eliminate eggs from the diet, buy only those that are guaranteed to have come from cage free farms that feed the hens only vegetarian and organic foods.

4. Be cautious in fish selection - Though we all know that some fish are full of beneficial "omega 3" oils, there are also some that are not so healthy because of mercury or fat content. Also, any farm-raised fish is not likely to be a good choice as well. The Monterey Bay Aquarium suggest eating the following fish as the "greenest" options: Albacore Tuna caught in the U.S. or British Columbia; Freshwater Coho Salmon from the U.S., Oysters, Pacific caught

Sardines, Rainbow Trout, and wild caught Alaskan Salmon. (Monterey Bay Aquarium, 2012).

Making these changes in your regular diet will really help to transition from the flexitarian to the purely plant based lifestyle. You will become far more conscientious about your choices and far more aware of the impact on your body and the environment. It takes some time, and that is why we also emphasize the need to move slowly from a diet with lots of meat and dairy to one that is all about plant based food.

One of the simplest methods used to do this is to start with one meatless day each week or one meatless meal each day. After accomplishing a week or two successfully, you can shift to two meals per day or two days per week that are entirely plant based, etc.

What is so interesting is that even once you are a full blown plant based eater, you can still put yourself into a few different categories. These include:

- Vegan - This is someone who includes absolutely no animal foods at all in the diet, including honey or beneficial bacteria.

- Fruitarian - Someone who consumes mostly fruit.

- Raw eater - Someone who tries to maintain the nutrient value of food by eating things uncooked or minimally heated.

- Macrobiotic - This is not truly a plant based eater because the true macrobiotic diet contains seafood.

- Nutritarian - This is someone who looks first at the micronutrients in their food and seeks to optimize the nutritional value of their diet on a per calorie basis. For example, they determine how many calories are needed in a meal and then eat the foods that supply those calories, but with an emphasis on the nutrient levels as well.

We give you these examples only to illustrate the great diversity of options open to someone who has decided to improve their health, reduce the size of their carbon footprint, help the planet, show compassion towards animals, and even lose a bit of weight by shifting to the plant based diet.

STEP BY STEP:
MOVING TOWARD A PLANT BASED DIET

With a much clearer understanding of what it means to be a plant based eater, you can now decide how and when to make the change. We are going to provide you with some tips and tactics that can make this a much easier thing to accomplish. As we already stated, it is a good idea to make this sort of change gradually in order to avoid "burn out".

For example, if it is too radical of a change from the way you normally eat, you will find yourself constantly thinking, worrying, and planning. This is not something that you will sustain on a permanent basis - no one can. Thus, if you really want to make the changes permanent, you have to do them slowly and in planned stages.

It is also a good idea to do this sort of change slowly because the plant based diet is very high in fiber, and this can often lead some unsuspecting individuals to experience great discomfort. Insoluble fiber is often a source of intestinal gas and can lead someone unused to such foods to experience bloating, flatulence, and digestive trouble.

So, follow the steps and tips below, and you should be able to claim to be a plant based eater in no time!

1. Cut out the meat slowly - We already discussed the idea of a "meatless" day or at least one meatless meal each day, but if you are currently eating the SAD it is likely that you are eating meat at each meal of the day. A recent article in the New York Times indicated that Americans eat an average of 200 pounds of meat per year - without adding in the dairy and the eggs. This translates to 110 grams or protein on any given day, but is an amount that is twice the suggested intake. With more than 75 grams of meat or animal protein in the average diet, it can be tough to just eliminate it, but you do need to start slowly dropping consumption to around 30 grams instead.

   This tells us that it is probably going to be tough for the "average" person to eliminate meat and dairy entirely and immediately. So, just start with the meat. Most recommend something like a "Meatless Monday", or a week that eliminates all of the meat from breakfast. It is just as effective to choose one type of meat to eliminate as well. For instance, you might decide to start the process by getting rid of all sources of red meat in your diet. A week or two later you could then remove the chicken or poultry, and so on.

   The thing to keep in mind here is that you have to do all of this at a pace that works for your needs. If you are feeling "deprived" of something, it is likely that you will not be able to successfully eliminate it permanently.

Also, be aware of the fact that a lot of people unknowingly replace the lost protein with starchy foods in order to get the same feeling of "fullness". While it may seem okay to add grains or potatoes in place of a chunk of meat, it is going to give you very little nutrition and fail to provide the body with what it needs.

Instead, replace the meat with a valid protein substitute.

2.   Eliminate dairy foods - This is often far more challenging than eliminating the meat. We eat dairy in ways that we may not even realize. That pat of butter on the morning toast, that dash of parmesan on the plate of pasta, or the bit of creamer in the coffee are all sources of dairy foods. Because of that, we suggest that you use the same approach to dairy elimination as used for meats.

1.   Start with a single dairy free day each week and then gradually expand on that theme;

2.   Start with a single dairy free meal each day, and then move on to a dairy free day;

3.   Pick one type of dairy food, such as cheese, and eliminate that entirely from the diet over the course of a few weeks, and then move on to the next, such as milk or yogurt;

4.   Find excellent substitutes and just make the switch. Soy yogurt, vegetable margarine, nut milks, and many other food choices can allow you to cut the dairy all at once. Remember, however, that cooking with these foods may require some experimentation to get the results desired. You also want to read the labels and watch the calories, fat, etc.

3.   Cut the eggs - This is often the last big hurtle to a plant based diet.

After all, eggs are such an easy and reliable food source, but the problem is that they are never an environmentally friendly or cruelty free food source. This means that they must go! This is not something done in "stages" like so many other food sources. Instead, it is usually done by committing to an egg free diet. There are some substitutes, but many use egg whites. Read the labels and start experimenting with alternatives when baking or cooking. For example, when eggs are used in baked goods they are often meant to serve as leavening or binding, and that means that a traditional egg substitute (sold in the dairy sections of most supermarkets) will work well. If you want to make something like a quiche, however, it will require a food that is close in texture to the finished product. This would be the time to experiment with tofu.

4. Start adding whole and unprocessed foods to the diet - If you are currently following the SAD, it means that you are probably not eating the suggested servings of fresh fruits and vegetables each day. To begin getting accustomed to the plant based diet may be as easy as adding a small green salad, some cooked green and red vegetables to that plate of whole wheat pasta, and shifting from processed breakfast cereals to rolled oats cooked into a nice oatmeal. It, of course, may not be that easy because you may not be used to many of the foods considered "whole" and unprocessed. For example, many people find tempeh, seitan, and piles of protein heavy beans a bit unusual when they are suddenly used to replace a beef patty or a piece of chicken. It is also a strange experience for those used to heavily salted and roasted nuts to start eating them

raw and unprocessed too.

This simply means that as you remove some of the foods from your usual diet, try to find creative ways to replace them with whole and unprocessed foods. That leads us to the need to start gathering recipes, which is the next "tip".

5. Gather recipes, gear, and experiment in the kitchen - A lot of people who have successfully shifted from a meat eating diet to a plant based one will tell you that they had to re-learn cooking, food prep, and shopping because they were unfamiliar with the many different textures, flavors, and techniques available. This means that you should:

    1. Start with a "recipe collection" - Whether this is a folder, binder, or entire box of recipes, the important thing is to stockpile a lot of resources and start experimenting with them. For instance, you might make a folder for many different categories, such as main dishes, desserts, snacks, etc. You can then narrow the group of recipes down to the "definitive" ones that work for you and your family. As an example, let's say that you want to avoid cooking for yourself and then cooking a separate meal for the family or for friends. The dilemma is that you know that something like macaroni and cheese is a real favorite. So, start seeking out alternatives using the Internet, the farmer's market, and any cooking demonstrations you witness.

        This becomes a very inspiring resource and a go-to solution, but it also helps to get you off to a great start with the plant based diet because it allows you to try new foods, new types of cuisine, and to use gear that you may not have used before. Think of such kitchen equipment as woks, high powered blenders for smoothies, and stackable steamers, etc.

6. Find role models, inspiration, and "network connections" - In this age of the Internet you can easily find hundreds of recipes, but you can also find a lot of ready answers from food experts and enthusiasts too. Go ahead and search a place like Facebook for plant based dieters, or the types of eaters you have chosen to become (remember that you might have opted to eat only raw foods or to eat mostly fruits, etc.). Join all of the groups that seem like a good fit and begin interacting with the community. Many of these people are happy to share recipes, resources for exotic or unusual ingredients, and to support you through your struggles when transitioning into this new lifestyle.

7. Shop for new gear - The plant based diet requires a lot of chopping, slicing, and other techniques. Why not treat yourself to some great knives, a high quality blender or food processor, and any other gear you have found that you need?

8. Expect and accept failure - Not to put a damper on your growing enthusiasm towards the plant based diet, but you will find that there are times when it is impossible to avoid the occasional "slip" or eating the "wrong" things. Expect this, accept it, and move on. Need an example? You may be asked for a meal at a friend's home, and they may ask you to bring something like a dessert or a salad. You decide that this is a great chance to introduce everyone to just

how delicious meat and dairy free foods can be. Everyone dives in and loves what you made, but the rest of the meal includes ample amounts of dairy and some meat. You are forced, partially out of politeness and partially out of a desire to do so, to eat servings of these forbidden foods.

It is okay; don't give up your plans because of a slip. The same thing goes for the times when you are at a restaurant that is unable to accommodate your need for dairy and meat free foods. It is a matter of just doing the best that you can and continuing forward along the path to better health and an environmentally friendly lifestyle.

If you are a parent and live with other people, it is highly likely that you may be unable to recruit them into your chosen lifestyle, and that can make it very challenging. Rather than facing the risks and temptations at each meal, the savvy plant based eater plans their meals and makes a few easy to reheat selections when it is time to sit down with the rest of the family, friends, or anyone else.

That last point brings us to a very significant issue, and that is "planning". The next chapter is going to really help you to succeed in making the change from the meat based eater to the plant based one. It is going to focus on the things you can do to ensure you make and eat only the healthiest, plant based foods and meals possible.

Before we head into that section, however, let's take a moment to consider the concept of planning.

PLANNING TO BE A PLANT BASED EATER

What sort of planning are we talking about here? If we are going to continue on with the theme of "step by step" methods to changing the diet, we have to actually go all of the way back to the beginning. This is because you may want to create a few deadlines for your chosen goals.

Just consider that we have indicated the need to shift to one meatless day each week or to one meatless meal each day. When will you begin to do this? When will you expand your efforts beyond the single day or meal? This points to the need for a calendar or a list of dates and plans. Consider the very workable template below:

1. Date to begin meatless day/meal:
2. Date to add another meatless day/meal:
3. Date to remove one type of meat from the diet:
4. Date to remove another meat from the diet:
5. Date to add one dairy-free day/meal:
6. Date to add another dairy-free day/meal:
7. Date to remove one type of dairy from the diet:

8. Date to remove another dairy from the diet:

9. Date to eliminate eggs from the diet:

In addition to such simple plans, you also have to consider any of the substitutes you intend to use, when you will add more whole and unprocessed foods to the diet, what sorts of recipes you will start with, which recipes you want to use on a regular basis, and when you will shop for gear and unique ingredients.

That is a lot of planning, but it will be very useful to you as you begin to shift into this new lifestyle. We recommend the use of a notebook or planner to help you track the dates and deadlines, to jot down notes about recipes or foods that you have liked or disliked, and to begin tracking your success and any challenges.

Now that you have an idea of how to use planning to your advantage we can go ahead and put your plans into action!

PLANT BASED GUIDELINES

We have already gone over the food groups, but to be sure you understand how to put this information to use, consider the following:

- Don't fill your plate with grains and starches. Try to cover any plate with two-thirds fruits and vegetables, and one third in protein, fat, and grains. Many folks make the mistake of filling up on starch and fat when they lose the protein, but that is a mistake. Instead, choose protein substitutes or use your veggies to "create" protein (see the last bullet point for details).

- Try to eat a rainbow and consume at least five servings of colorful fruits and vegetables every single day.

- Do eat at least six servings of grains, tubers, or legumes each day in order to regulate blood sugar and provide adequate energy.

- Stop buying processed foods of any kind and skip the sugar and salt.

- Remember that fruit or vegetable smoothies and shakes are a very easy and filling way to get your necessary nutrients, fiber, and food.

- Combine foods to create good protein and fat combinations. For example, a salad or side dish that uses green beans, barley, and almonds makes a complete protein! To help with this issue we provide a table below, but it is fairly easy to find your favorite combinations by experimenting over time.

It is really that simple, but you do have to start to think like an artist and have the necessary materials at hand in order to begin making your masterpieces of nutrition. Before we head to the formal shopping list, let's take a moment to explore those protein combinations.

PERFECT PROTEIN COMBINATIONS

In order to allow foods to blend together and to create perfect protein (think any combination of seeds, nuts, and legumes OR any combination of legumes and whole grains) you have to also consider their individual properties. The basic "formula" is to use a primary food that is low in sulfur, a secondary food that is low in tryptophan, and a third food that is low in lysine.

The following foods will combine to create complete proteins:

- Green beans + barley + almonds
- Broccoli + chard + pecans (roasted or unroasted)
- Asparagus + mushrooms + roasted pumpkin seeds
- Soybeans +brown rice + corn
- Lentils + garbanzo beans+ brown rice
- Potatoes + green peas + yams

Do you see how any of these might combine to create delicious meals? We provide some recipes below, but you will also want to experiment with these combinations on your own. Remember that the foods are listed in order of priority, or quantity. Thus, the lentils, garbanzos and brown rice would use much less rice than the soybeans, brown rice, and corn, etc.

Now that you are fully armed with all of the details required to begin making plans for your transition to a plant based diet, we can get you fully prepared with a comprehensive shopping list, some sample menus, and few very reliable and delicious recipes!

SHOPPING LIST

By no means do you have to buy all of the things listed here, but if you have taken our advice and started jotting down some plans and deadlines for yourself, it is likely that you also see that you are going to need a much more plant based pantry very soon. Use the list of foods below to be sure that you have the basics, as well as some nice extras, in order to really support your efforts.

Remember that some of these specialty foods are a bit costly, and you may want to purchase them in bulk (things like nuts and seeds are often best purchased in large quantities and frozen), store them properly, and use them as needed. For instance, many people head to warehouse stores like Costco to stock up on raw nuts, frozen berries, and high quality vegetables. They then divide them up and freeze them for slow and affordable consumption.

When it is a matter of purchasing such things as herbs or spices, just add one or two bottles or packages to the cart each week. Doing this allows you to affordably update the pantry and provides you with some new flavors to explore. For instance, if you have never made any sort of "curry" dish, you will want to explore the recipes and purchase the costly ingredients over one or two week's time, and then use these specialty foods each time you whip up a batch of healthy curry in the future.

Also remember to seek out organic foods whenever you can find and afford them!

Protein Sources:

- Soy products:
  - Tofu
  - Seitan
  - Tempeh
  - TVP
  - Soy milk
  - Soy yogurt
  - Soy based cheeses
  - Soy ice cream
- Nuts and seeds:
  - Nut butters of any kind (make sure there are no added sugars and that the butter is not hydrogenated in any way)
  - Tahini
  - Any type of unsalted and raw nuts (roasting can be done at home and will help preserve the nutrient content)
  - Any type of unsalted and plain seeds (you will often find seed flours like flax, etc.)

- Legumes (Beans are inexpensive, but can increase in price substantially when purchased pre-cooked in cans. Though this makes it easy to use them, it reduces their nutritional value and provides too much sodium. Stick with the dried beans whenever possible, and simply soak overnight before using them):
  - All types of dried beans (including lentils, split peas, and "blends")
  - Frozen beans, but remember that limas are much higher in starch than others.

Fruits:

It is impossible to provide a comprehensive list of all fruits on the market. What we can tell you is that you want to consider fresh, frozen, and dried:

- Dried fruits should have no added sugar and no sulfur. Good choices include dates, cranberries, raisins, pineapple, cherries, figs, and prunes, among others.
- Frozen fruits should also have no added sugar and no preservatives. Organic is the best way to go, particularly with strawberries. This is a good option when it is not the growing season and fresh fruits are much higher in price.
- Preserves and butters can be chosen as well, just be sure they are no to low sugar varieties that use whole fruits. These are great sweeteners for baking too!
- Fruit nectars that include only 100% juice

Vegetables:

Again, just like fruit, it is not possible to create a complete list of all vegetables available to consumers. This means you want to explore your options for fresh and frozen foods, and always organic when available.

- Frozen vegetables should have no additives or preservatives, and minimal processing. This is a good option when it is not the growing season and fresh vegetables are much higher in price.

- Sauces and canned products such as ketchup, tomato paste, marinara, salsa, and other similar items should be low sodium and organic.

Whole Grains and Starches:

- Amaranth

- Brown Basmati rice

- Brown rice

- Millet

- Quinoa

- Wild rice

- Buckwheat flour

- Brown rice flour

- Quinoa pasta

- Rice noodles

- Whole Wheat flour

- Whole wheat noodles and pasta

- Oatmeal

- Whole grain crackers

- Popcorn
- Whole grain tortillas and "wraps"
- Whole grain corn chips

Fats:

- Oils that are cold pressed are the best, particularly with olive and canola oils.
- Sesame oil is great when it is made from dark and toasted seeds.

All of the Rest:

- Tea and coffee
- Herbal tea
- Vinegars - balsamic, cider, red and white, rice, and those seasoned with herbs or fruit
- Coconut products such as milk, shredded and flaked meat, etc.
- Tamari
- A diversity of dried herbs and spices (fresh herbs are nice to grow on a windowsill too!)
- Fresh ginger root
- Salt substitutes
- Nutritional yeast
- Seaweed sheets to add to soup or to even make sushi
- Mustard (low sodium)
- Pure maple syrup
- Broths made without salt and organic

- Pickled foods that provide beneficial bacteria (remember, you are not eating yogurt but many fermented foods provide similar benefits)

As you can see, you may have many of these foods already filling your cupboards and shelves. Go ahead now and do an inventory. Make a detailed list of the things you know you will eat. If you are still a bit "stumped", just take a peek at some of our sample daily menus to help you determine the types of things you will be making in the coming days and weeks.

SAMPLE MENUS

So, how do you begin eating the plant based diet? You make those plans we already mentioned, and then you start experimenting with ingredients and recipes of all kinds. We also suggested that you take a look at food colors to get all of your phytonutrients as well, which means trying to eat a rainbow of colors each day.

"That's all fine and dandy," you might reasonably say, "but just how do I combine all of this information into a healthy and fulfilling way of eating?"

Use some of the sample menus below to guide your initial choices. It won't take you long to identify your particular favorites and to begin learning which foods you prefer, and at which meals you prefer to eat them.

BREAKFAST SUGGESTIONS

- Whole grain cereal with serving of fruit and a milk substitute (for example, organic shredded wheat cereal with a sliced banana and soy milk OR organic whole grain corn flakes with strawberries and almond milk);

- Oatmeal with serving of fruit and nuts (for example, organic rolled oats cooked with water and served with sliced banana and pecans OR organic rolled oats cooked with soy milk and served with sliced peaches and chopped almonds);

- Breakfast burritos made with whole grain tortillas or wraps and filled with an egg replacement and soy cheese OR tofu sausage and vegetables OR a combination of these things;

- Whole grain pancakes or waffles topped with a serving of fruit (organic frozen blueberries are great, but so too would be anything from bananas or peaches to fresh strawberries) and maple/agave/honey OR you could use a nut butter and honey instead of the fruit;

- Whole grain toast with nut butter and a serving of soy yogurt with fruit;

- Classic breakfast of eggs and bacon using veggie substitutes, serve with whole grain toast;

- Breakfast muffins - banana muffins are great, but you can find bran muffins, apple cinnamon muffins, and classic blueberry muffin recipes that all use plant based ingredients;

- Eggless omelet with mixed vegetables and whole grain toast with vegetable margarine; or

- A smoothie using fruits, vegetables, and protein.

LUNCH SUGGESTIONS

NOTE: You want to always try to make a good blend of foods at lunch, and include a serving of fruit and a small serving of protein such as some hummus or tofu cheese, peanut butter or nut butter, etc.

- Homemade soup that uses at least one full serving of vegetables and/or whole grain pasta OR serve it with whole grain crackers;

- Whole grain wrap with hummus and vegetables OR meat substitute and veggie cheese OR a combination of all;

- Large lentil or bean salad (include a full serving of vegetables) with a cup of brown rice or a whole grain bread;

- Fruit salad with soy yogurt and whole grain granola;

- Traditional sandwich of any kind as long as it uses whole grain bread, vegetarian meat substitutes, and organic condiments;

- Veggie burger on a whole wheat roll with salad on the side;

- Baked potato with vegetarian chili (use a recipe that require protein substitute such as TVP and beans) and some veggie or soy cheese;

- Whole grain wraps filled with at least one cup of vegetables, and any toppings that provide a good balance - could be hummus, tahini, veggie cheese, etc.;

- Assorted raw vegetables with dip (could be made using soy yogurt, soy based creamy cheese, hummus, etc.), whole grain crackers, and fruit; or

- Leftovers from dinner OR Breakfast for Lunch!

DINNER SUGGESTIONS

Just like dinner, you want to be sure that you are balancing out the meal with plenty of fruits and vegetables and also eating a good serving of protein. Dinner is also the "classic" meal for adding a tossed salad or fruit cup as well.

- Whole grain pasta with vegetables in a vegetable cheese dressing and a small salad;

- Homemade chili that uses TVP (or another protein substitute), a large green salad, whole grain bread, small fruit cup;

- Eggplant or vegetable "parmesan", steamed vegetables seasoned with lemon, whole grain bread or pasta;

- Whole grain pizza topped with anything you want and served with a large side salad;

- Stir fry using at least two servings of vegetables and served with brown rice;

- A "perfect protein" meal (we provide two excellent recipes below, but you can also refer to the combinations on page 32 to create your own unique dishes;

- Pot pies that use vegetable and protein substitute bases and either mashed potatoes or a whole grain biscuit mixture for the "crust" along with a large tossed salad;

- Veggie burgers of any kind served on whole grain rolls with "oven baked" fries and a nice big salad;

- Tex Mex food that uses whole grain tortillas or romaine leaves as "wraps" for everything from lentil filled tacos to chili stuffed quesadillas;

- Classic homemade soup and salad with whole grain bread or crackers;

- Casseroles using whole grain "bases" such as brown rice or whole wheat pasta, and partnered with beans and veggies to create ideal protein combinations; or

- Breakfast for Dinner!

Clearly, this is just the proverbial tip of the iceberg, and we would like to help you to get things off to a good start by providing some timeless recipes that you will use over and over again.

TOP RECIPES

PERFECT PROTEIN POTATOES AND PEAS

Serves 6

Ingredients:

2 cloves garlic, minced

3 tbsp. olive oil

1/4 cup parsley, chopped

10 new potatoes (red or white skin), cleaned and cut into chunks

2 yams or sweet potatoes, cleaned and cut into chunks

Salt and pepper, to taste

3 cups of frozen petite peas, defrosted in a colander

1/4 cup chopped scallions (including the greens)

1 cup of unroasted, raw pecans, chopped

Directions:

Heat the oven to 375 and prepare a large oblong baking pan by spraying it with cooking oil. In a bowl, combine the garlic, oil, parsley and salt and pepper. Toss in potatoes and yams, toss to coat with mixture and then pour them into the prepared pan. Bake this for 30 minutes, or until potatoes are tender. Stir in the peas and green onions and gently toss. Bake for five to ten minutes and then taste for seasoning. Garnish with the pecans and serve.

PERFECT PROTEIN MUSHROOM ASPARAGUS TOSS

Serves 6

Ingredients

1/4 cup roasted pumpkin seeds

Salt and pepper to taste

1 pound of sliced mushrooms (button mushrooms are best for this)

Zest and juice of one large lemon

2 pounds of fresh asparagus, trimmed

Olive oil

Directions:

Heat the olive oil in a large skillet and add the pumpkin seeds, salt, and pepper. Toast them for about three minutes and set aside. Add more oil to the pain and cook the mushrooms over medium heat until they release their fluids and turn brown (this will take around five minutes). Add the mushrooms to the bowl with the pumpkin seeds. Add the remaining olive oil to the pan and stir in the lemon juice. Add the asparagus and cook until tender about four minutes. Return the seeds and mushrooms to the pan and heat through. Season with salt and pepper and add the lemon zest for extra flavor.

AMAZING SMOOTHIE

Serves 1

1/4 cup almonds soaked overnight in water

1/2 fresh pear or 1/2 cup of fresh blueberries

1 banana

2 cups of water or 1 1/2 cups of water with one cup of ice)

Serving of any vegan protein powder (chocolate flavor is amazing with this recipe)

Directions

Add everything to your blender or smoothie maker and you have an instant meal!

GREEN SMOOTHIE FOR A PLANT BASED EATER

Rather than give you a single recipe, we will give you an optimal "formula". You choose one food source from the first list and then add any combination of additional items from the next. You will have to add a bit of juice, water, ice, or soy/nut milk to complete the process. Use one serving of any of the foods chosen for a single smoothie, and double up if you are making a batch for yourself and a friend!

Choose from the following:

Lettuce

Kale

Watercress

Turnip or mustard greens

Broccoli

Asparagus

Collard greens

Kohlrabi

Celery

Then add any combination from the following (but use only half servings for these):

Banana

Apple

Pear

Orange

Mango

Papaya

Pineapple

Kiwi

Berries of any kind

Watermelon

Cucumber

Put these into the blender with your choice of juice, water, ice or milk substitute and you will have an impressively green and healthy smoothie that can be used as a meal substitute or as a good way to get your daily servings of fruits and vegetables.

TOP OF THE LINE VEGGIE CHILI

Serves 6

Ingredients

6 cups of cooked beans, any kind you prefer

1 medium onion, diced

3 ripe tomatoes, diced

1/2 cup diced hot peppers

8 ounce can of organic tomato sauce

1/s cup chili powder

1 tsp garlic powder

1 tsp cumin

1 tsp paprika

Salt and pepper to taste, or a squeeze of lime juice

Directions

In a large sauce pan add the beans, onion, fresh tomato, hot peppers, and can of sauce. Cook until the vegetables have softened. Stir in the spices and taste. Adjust as needed and then continue to simmer slowly until most of the fluids have evaporated. Be sure to keep the temperatures low to avoid burning. This freezes well and you can easily make a double batch and put half away for later consumption.

CLASSIC BLUEBERRY MUFFINS

Makes 12

Ingredients

1 cup homemade applesauce or an organic brand from the jar

1/2 raw sugar

2 ripe bananas, mashed and set aside

1 tbsp almond milk

1 tsp pure vanilla extract

1 tsp baking soda

1/4 tsp salt

2 cups whole wheat pastry flour

1 cup fresh or frozen blueberries

1/2 cup nuts (walnuts are great in this recipe)

Directions

Preheat the oven to 350 and prepare a classic muffin tin. In a large bowl combine the applesauce and sugar. Stir in the bananas, milk, and vanilla, and mix again. Stir in the soda, salt, and the whole wheat flour, and stir to blend well. Add the nuts and carefully fold the blueberries into the batter (you may want to freeze them to make this easier). Drop batter into the prepared pan, filling each cup around 3/4 full. Bake for 25 minutes, or until they test well with a toothpick. Remove from the oven and allow to cool in the pan. (You can also grease a traditional loaf pan and bake this into a bread for 40 minutes)

You can adjust this recipe to include other fruits instead of the blueberries, just be aware of the change in fluid levels. For example, some additional mashed bananas, some chopped apples with a dash of cinnamon, and even strawberries could all create wonderful results.

PLANT BASED CASEROLE

This is a great way to create another perfect protein, and makes a wonderful pot luck contribution too. Who needs old fashioned mac and cheese when this dish is available!

Ingredients

3 cups water

1 cup brown rice

1 8 oz can of organic tomato sauce

2 cups cooked pinto and black beans.

1 cup fresh or frozen organic corn

1 tsp salt

1 tsp onion powder

1 tsp chili powder

1/2 tsp garlic powder

1/2 tsp cumin

Directions

Preheat oven to 350 and prepare a 9x15 casserole with a bit of cooking spray. Stir all of the ingredients directly into the prepared pan. Bake, uncovered for 1 1/2 hours, but be sure the rice has become tender. (You can also do this on the stove top by using 2 1/2 cups of water in a skillet, covering it tightly and cooking over medium heat for the same amount of time.)

Check on the dish while it is cooking and add water if needed. Allow to cool a bit before serving. It is great with avocado and salsa, but also makes a fine sandwich filling or wrap.

UNIVERSAL CHEESE SAUCE

Most plant based eaters say that they quickly come to miss cheese based sauces for dishes like macaroni and cheese or as a topping for chili or steamed vegetables. This sauce is a delicious alternative, and is even gluten free too!

Ingredients

1/4 cup "nutritional yeast"

2 Tbsp wheat flour

1/2 tsp onion powder

1/2 tsp garlic powder

1/4 tsp turmeric

1/2 tsp salt, or to taste

1/4 tsp cumin (for a Tex Mex flavor)

1/2 tsp chili powder (for a Tex Mex flavor)

1 cup unsweetened rice, soy or almond milk

Directions

Add all of the dry ingredients to a medium saucepan over medium heat. Whisk them as they begin to heat and toast, but be careful that they don't burn. Once they are fragrant and warm begin to slowly stir in the milk. Keep stirring as you slowly pour the milk into the pan and then continue to stir until it is thick. Experiment with seasonings to create a Mexican cheese topping, a less spicy topping, etc.

This is great on veggies, stirred into leftover casseroles, over hot potatoes, and even on traditional corn chip "nachos".

DAILY VEGGIE SALAD

Serves 4

Ingredients

Bunch of scallions, chopped with greens

4 Tbsp olive oil

Juice of one lemon

Two cloves garlic

Small bunch parsley, basil, marjoram, thyme, and rosemary

1 tsp red pepper flakes

Large red pepper, seeded and chopped

Large cucumber, chopped

Bunch of radishes, cleaned and chopped

3 cups mixed greens

1/2 cup chopped fresh black olives

Pint cherry tomatoes, chopped

Directions

Place all of the vegetables into a large salad bowl. Take the herbs, the garlic, the oil, and the lemon juice and puree into a loose paste. Put this on top of the mixed vegetables. Toss, adding additional lemon juice and oil if necessary, and season with salt and pepper to taste.

IN CONCLUSION

It is impossible to sum up your plant based diet with a word. It is not simply "meatless" or "vegetarian". It is more of a lifestyle than anything else because it is chosen by many people who want to enjoy a long list of benefits.

Consider that you will be able to eliminate or reduce some very problematic health issues when you eliminate animal fats, processed grains, and sugars from the diet. You will lose weight, see a dip in blood pressure, and even get high cholesterol under control.

Additionally, you will be able to choose from an array of food sources that is nearly endless. You, quite literally, have a world of foods and flavors in front of you when you choose the plant based diet.

Experimentation is going to be a key to success, but keep in mind that you need to set goals and to make the shift slowly. Don't burn out by trying too hard and being too tough on yourself. Don't focus on the things you can't eat when you can instead think about all the delicious foods that you can eat!

Use the resources available here and also remember to do a lot of social networking with your fellow plant based eaters. They are great resources for recipes and ideas, and they can really encourage and support you as you begin to eat in the healthiest way possible!

THANKS FOR READING!

If you've enjoyed this book please be sure to check out my other books:

Raw Food Diet for Beginners

Smoothies Recipes for Beginners

Juicing Recipes for Beginners

Vegan Recipes for Beginners

Vegetarian Recipes for Beginners

DASH Diet for Beginners

Also, please take a moment to leave a review for us on Amazon. Your feedback helps to improve this and future books.

Good luck and healthy eating!

Made in the USA
Middletown, DE
10 October 2017